LOOKING BACK

GROWING UP IN EAST LONDON
1918–1939

By Eric Dawson

"As Mrs Corck, a friend of my mother remarked, it was as if there had always been war; the time between the wars we had looked upon as peace was an unreal dream."

LOOKING BACK

GROWING UP IN EAST LONDON
1918–1939

By Eric Dawson

Published by the London Borough of Newham 2006

Designed by Good Impressions

ISBN 0-9543224-1-X

INTRODUCTION

Newham Council has published this memoir by Eric Dawson in acknowledgement of his most generous gift of 42 paintings depicting West Ham between 1918, the year of Eric's birth, and 1939, the year he joined the army. Following his retirement from work as a freelance graphic designer in 1988, he began to record his memories of his boyhood and early manhood in a series of watercolours.

Looking Back is a record, in his own words, of Eric Dawson's own life and of the lives of his extended family and friends between the two World Wars. Eric was born at the very end of the First World War and never knew his father who died following a gas attack in the trenches. In this illustrated account of his early years, he evokes a comfortable but not overly wealthy Forest Gate of close-knit families and helpful neighbours. There are some chain stores on the busier streets but every neighbourhood has its small privately owned shops – butcher, grocer, sweet shop, boot and shoe repairer, oil shop - providing necessities on a daily basis. Sunday Schools and Temperance meetings attract large audiences and it is not unusual for a cinema to seat 3,000 people. At home, evening parties include poetry recitals and songs around the piano. He describes families travelling on the criss-cross of local railway lines to spend holidays at seaside resorts where the lodgings are modest but the home cooking superb. But these are not untroubled times as news of crises abroad force the recognition that another war is on its way.

He brings to life his gregarious grandfather, his hard-working and talented mother and a host of other family members, schoolteachers and friends. It is a record of the unique circumstances of his own life based in East London at a particular time in history. However, there are many aspects which will strike a chord with modern readers wherever they are and whatever their background – the struggles of his widowed mother to contribute to the household income whilst finding enough time for her young son, the trauma of serious childhood illness, the petty and not so petty humiliations of life in the classroom or gym, the embarrassments of adolescence and seemingly unavoidable misunderstandings between the sexes.

The places Eric describes are now part of Newham. The borough has seen a sharp fall in population and serious economic decline since Eric's time. But the 20th century also saw new communities moving in and government-supported funding to underpin economic regeneration. A great deal has changed in the West Ham, Stratford and Forest Gate of the 21st century but there is much in Eric's reminiscences that all who live there today can recognise and enjoy.

LIST OF ILLUSTRATIONS

PROLOGUE

Letters dated 9/10 September 1918, addressed to my mother, sent from No 7 Casualty Clearing Station, British Expeditionary Force (BEF).

I remember, I remember, the house where I was born

ONE

In 1890, two brothers, joining an accelerating movement away from the overcrowded eastern districts of the City of London, left Bow for Forest Gate, then still retaining something of a rural atmosphere. They bought adjoining houses in Beauchamp Road, leasehold, for about £200 each. The elder brother was my grandfather, William Robert Buck, the other my great-uncle Arthur. Both were recently married.

My grandfather worked as a printer at Waterlows, in the City. In those days all business transactions were recorded by hand in large leather-bound ledgers. My grandfather was a "ruler", producing the lined sheets for these ledgers, horizontally for recording successive items, then overprinting vertical columns for the entry of pounds, shillings and pence. These cash columns were frequently printed in a variety of coloured inks, according to clients' individual requirements. When, on returning from work, my grandfather washed his hands in the tiny scullery, gorgeous soapy tints of the colours he had been using that day – carmine, ultramarine, purple, emerald – were released from his fingers, descending in lovely spirals down the plug hole in the earthenware sink.

A gregarious man of many interests, he was happiest in his home, surrounded by his family. My mother, recalling her own childhood, remembered him taking his supper in the warm crowded kitchen. A well-filled plate in front of him, a toddler on one knee, the cat at his feet. And from a distance of about 18 inches Daisy Tibbets watched every mouthful disappear. (Daisy was the daughter of a family lodging in two of the rooms upstairs. My mother considered she was a greedy child; perhaps she was just hungry). On one occasion my grandfather piled a fork high with an assortment of food and coaxed the contents into her mouth, watching with great amusement as she struggled to consume this overwhelming windfall.

Each house contained, on the upper floor, three small bedrooms and a bathroom, and downstairs an adjoining front and back reception room (the parlour) a small kitchen and a scullery. There was an outside toilet. Most rooms had fireplaces for coal fires. Lighting was by gas. There was no hot water.

The lifestyle enjoyed by the occupants of these two houses was sharply contrasted. For my grandparents, with a growing family of four children, life was a struggle. My grandmother assumed the responsibility of feeding and clothing her young brood, of eking out the money to last the week. She probably also had the worry of paying household bills. But my grandfather gloried in it. He sang his way through evenings and weekends with the popular ballads of the day, accompanying himself on the banjo, and, later, when funds ran to its acquisition, an upright cottage piano. His banjo playing was not in the conventional plinkety-plonk style associated with that instrument, but consisted of isolated dramatic chords punctuating the sung melody. Well, that was his aim, but in practice he sometimes groped for the chords, sadly holding up the flow of the song. His preferences lay towards the dramatic: *Trumpeter, what are you sounding now?* – valour in the battlefield, and in the final stirring call, resurrection of the fallen, or the *Death of Nelson*. Items such as these were not universally popular, particularly later on, after the First World War, when, to his incomprehension, my mother refused to stay in the room and listen to it.

Romantically, he loved to sing any song – and there were lots of them – which included his wife's name: Her name is Mary, the sweetest name I know which usually brought forth the impatient response: 'Oh get on with you, Will!' A fervent supporter of the British Empire, he gloried in national accomplishments. He had no time for the Kaiser, Bolsheviks, Trades Unions, Pacifists, Film Stars (but among entertainers George Robey, 'the honest vulgarian', was acceptable). Revelling in arguments, he could frequently be seen in animated disagreement with Uncle Tom, on the corner of Kitchener Road. (Uncle Tom was a die-hard Socialist, and even worse, a Free Thinker, and was unfortunately married to my grandfather's sister).

Having earlier in the day retrieved a copy of the *Morning Post* or even *The Times* from Waterlows, my grandfather's nightly task was to take pen and ink

Grandfather and Eric in the kitchen

down from the dresser in the kitchen, and copy out the leading article. Whether this was to reinforce his political beliefs, or to improve his mind, or just to assume some studious semblance of authorship, it is no longer possible to ascertain.

A picture hanging in the passage leading to the front door was a reproduction of Franz Hals' *The Laughing Cavalier.* As a small child I thought this had a remarkable likeness to my grandfather, except that my grandad had auburn hair and whiskers. Arthur and Alice lived next door in a house which was the mirror image of our own, but totally different in atmosphere. They were a childless couple. Arthur had a responsible job (also at Waterlows) and was of a quiet and serious disposition. Alice was a slight figure, fresh-faced with bright candid eyes, in some ways the embodiment of a model wife, industrious, a good manager, a painstaking cook. She also had a creative turn of mind and was given to learning and reciting great chunks of Victorian poetry. Longfellow was a great favourite, she would recite the saga of Hiawatha and his bride: 'By the waterfall he named her Minnehaha, Laughing Water'. In contrast, Arthur's one claim to fame was his ability to close one eye independently of the other. As a child I found this vastly intriguing, and would beg him to do it again, please.

Alice was an indefatigable correspondent, with a wide range of friends. Their home reflected the ordered tenure of their lives. Not knocked about, like ours. Paintwork immaculate ("cream-white, Arthur, please!"). All sash windows in perfect working order, Venetian blinds which went up and down evenly without sticking together. Furniture in Edwardian style, of good quality. Bright Turkey carpets, spotless lace starched curtains, gleaming brass rods on the stairs. A large harmonium with stops (vox humana), with inset engravings of cherubim and seraphim. A very tall upright piano with a green pleated silk front. Really well cared for aspidistras. Politically liberal, they had a framed photograph of Lloyd George hung in the kitchen. They were devout members of the local Baptist Church.

In the early days of the 1920s it seemed as if every other road in Forest Gate was lined with shops. The main thoroughfares, heavy with traffic, much of it still horse-drawn, contained the larger establishments – Woolworth's, The Penny Bazaar, Home and Colonial, the Co-op. Lots of dress-shops, haberdashers and milliners. Freeman Hardy and Willis (shoes), Montague Burton, 'the tailor of taste'.

The back streets provided the daily necessities of the local inhabitants. Just around the corner from us, in St George's Road, a group of such local shops existed. On the corner a haberdasher's owned and run by two refined maiden ladies. During my mother's dressmaking period I was frequently dispatched to buy some item she had, at that moment, run out of. A reel of Sylco in some specified colour, a penny packet of pins, or some tailoring chalk. A selection of ladies' and children's garments were on sale, together with knitting wools, dress patterns, embroidery threads, bright silken ribbons.

Green Street, Upton Park

Next door, a small laundry operated. Then came the Oil Shop, dark, aromatic, with bundles of chopped firewood ranged against the counter. A wide selection of household necessities, paints and distempers, wallpaper, candles, gas mantles, storm lanterns, tin kettles, zinc-fronted food safes, buckets, bath tubs, washing boards, scrubbing brushes, black lead, fly papers, whiting, augmented surprisingly by one or two comestible lines, for example vinegar dispensed into your own jug from wooden barrels, and, I seem to remember, treacle.

Next, another handy shop, the boot and shoe repairer. Humming with some mechanical activity, this service was operated by an amiable but quite spectacularly grimy individual named Caruthers, whose son was in my class at school. Exall, the grocer. Crowded counters piled high with almost everything to eat that you could think of, including cooked meats (brawn, faggots); the proprietor himself, a dignified man in an almost floor-length white apron, lovingly slicing a complete ham, which rested on a pink and white china pedestal. Mrs Exall operated the bacon-slicer, amid exotic ranges of slab cake. Biscuits were sold loose from large square tins.

The formidable and energetic Misses Prentiss ran the sweet shop. Acid drops at 2d a quarter, penny chocolate bars, boxed novelty assortments. Toffee in trays to be broken up weighed and dispensed in small paper bags. Strictly for children, half penny items of dubious origin, tiger nuts, locust beans, chinese coconut.

Forest Gate Sanitary Steam Laundry

Cigarettes (10 for 6d) and pipe tobacco. A wide counter laid out with newspapers and magazines. Fireworks in season. A Christmas club. Paxton, the butcher, the floorboards liberally sprinkled with sawdust. Mrs Paxton, ensconced in a glass cabinet, wrapping up the meat, receiving payment and dispensing change.

At the far corner of this little terrace of shops was the off-licence. Despite the fact that the off-licence was run by a very superior red-faced individual in black coat and striped trousers, it was considered by us to be rather less than respectable. On the rare occasions of a visit from Mrs Burton, an acquaintance of my grandmother's from Poplar, knowing her propensity for something a little stronger than a cup of tea, one of the youngsters would be despatched with a jug to the off-licence for a pint of stout. Back home, the whole family would watch the guest as she delicately raised the black veil on her hat to sip the beverage.

Within five minutes' walk was West Ham Park. Here we sped our scooters along smooth asphalt paths, and in summer learned to play cricket (underarm bowling) in the shade of large leafy chestnut trees. The flower gardens, splendidly maintained by the City of London, were patrolled by stern park-keepers with whistles. Close by was Upton Lane School, which all the family at various times attended. From our beds, in the early morning, we could hear the first trams screeching and clanking as they negotiated the sudden bend at the Spotted Dog.

Further north along Upton Lane, occupying a whole block, was the Forest Gate Sanitary Steam Laundry. This establishment ejected vast clouds of steam across Upton Lane; at night the dramatic effect was enhanced by powerful but flickering arc lights illuminating work areas. Sounds of heavy machinery rent the air, occasionally interspersed with women's voices raised in song, a truly Wagnerian manifestation. One winter's night when my grandmother and I were passing the laundry, a sudden gust of wind snatched her hat into the air and it disappeared behind the laundry's high brick wall. Seething with annoyance, my grandmother seized my arm and we sped off home, she most anxious to avoid being seen in this disreputable condition.

On the far side of West Ham Park was a large house called The Cedars, once the home of the Gurney family. It was now used by the local Territorials and by the British Legion, the ex-servicemen's club, very active in this period following the end of the First World War. The Legion announced an outing for war-orphans, a free journey by horse brake to a Retreat in Hainault Forest, where tea would be provided, and there would be free rides on roundabouts. My mother got to know about this and decided to let me go. Before we went, most surprisingly, she sewed all my father's medals, including his Croix de Guerre, on to my dark blue jersey. The effect was to turn me into something resembling a Christmas tree decoration, the glinting bronze and silver of the medals enhanced by the beautiful rainbow-like colours of the ribbons. I was then about five.

Outside The Cedars several horse brakes were drawn up, decorated over all with flowers and favours and were filling up with excited children, the atmosphere distinctly of the 'knees-up' variety. There were no medals and it seemed unlikely that any military decorum (if that was what my mother had anticipated) could be expected. Doubts crept into her mind – I was not to go. So we went home again.

The holidays enjoyed in this early part of my childhood usually meant staying with family friends, or joining relatives at some existing lodging. We had two such short holidays at Brighton in the immediate post-war years. Next to my mother in age was her brother Bill. Against all odds, as an infantry man, he had survived more or less intact, although at this time limping slightly from the effects of a leg wound. Having been forcibly removed from the family by his war service he now valued his independence, and had no intention of returning. Training to become (of all things!) a diamond cutter, he had taken a lodging in Brighton. In these liberated circumstances he enjoyed an enviable life-style, dominating his landlady and indulging in various weekend jaunts, which included popping up to London for an evening at the theatre.

The last workmen's train, Forest Gate Railway Station

The train to Margate

This was where we stayed. The lodging was fairly basic, and situated at the back of the town, perhaps for the convenience of the landlady's rarely seen husband, an engine driver apparently on permanent night duty. Meal times varied depending on what time Bill deigned to return to the house. Once we were joined by my mother's sister Elsie and her dashing ex-serviceman suitor (another William, mercifully known as Billy) who due to lack of room were boarded out in spare accommodation in a neighbour's house. Great fun ensued, as with the baby in a hired pushchair, the party tramped across rain-sodden Downs. After an evening meal ("Would you like a nice piece of steak, Bill?") we were out again, sampling the delights of the Town. My mother wrapped up her sleeping small charge, and trundled it off to the Pier, where she found a nice place out of the wind and settled down with an interesting book.

We shared a semi-basement room which had a window at pavement level. Inside, beneath the window, was the usual wash-hand stand with ewer and basin. There was a sort of ledge above on which was propped a photograph, taken during the war, of the landlady's son, which we seemed to be continually knocking down into the soapy water. When this happened my mother would wipe him down, and with a brief apology, return him to the ledge.

At five years of age I joined the Infants' Department at Upton Lane School. Of this period I have very little recall except that my class teacher, Miss

Twentymen, kept in her desk, as a reward for exceptionally good behaviour, a jar of yellow boiled sweets. By nature very good at a ploy like this, I soon became a regular recipient. Being forbidden to consume the reward in class, and anxious anyway to share to occasion with my mother, I would rush home after school with the prize firmly gripped in my handkerchief. There, unable to wait even until the front door was opened, I would shout my good news through the letter box.

At seven we transferred to the Big Boys. Here we sat in rows of indestructably solid desks, the tops of which were hinged to open up as a book rest. Discipline was quite strict, corporal punishment being dispensed on the spot, the cane resting conveniently near the teacher's desk. Having already absorbed the

The Balaam Street Baths, Plaistow

rudiments of reading and writing, our lessons now became more complicated. Text books appeared, we composed our first essays, in our own exercise books. On the wall maps of the world displayed all the countries in different colours but the British Empire, one quarter of the world's surface, was shown in pink.

Occasionally we left school for an outside period. A real treat was to visit Balaam Street swimming baths in Plaistow. We travelled by tram, rushing to the upper deck. Under our arms we carried rolled-up towels containing our bathing costumes. An abiding recollection of these visits is a fusion of noise, colour, smell and movement – vociferous shrieks from the over-excited small boys echoing off tiles and agitated water, a green glow, an overriding smell of chlorine.

At ten, I entered Standard 4. This was the class which would provide candidates for the once-only chance of gaining a scholarship to the West Ham Secondary School; about 100 places were available. Our school work became more intensive, now under the guidance of our new teacher, Mr Hughes. When the day of the examinations arrived, my mother went with me up the passage to the front door. Straightening my cap, she said, "Now don't you worry about anything. Just do your best."

For two hours or so I was absorbed in answering the questions placed before us. Home again, normal life resumed. About six weeks later I learned that I had gained 67th place in the examinations, and in September would be leaving Upton Lane School for good.

About ten of us in the class had passed. Mr Hughes arranged for a group photograph of us to be taken, a boy sitting in the middle of the centre row bearing a slate which read: "1929 Scholarship Winners".

Four schoolboys, each with a penn'orth of chips

TWO

I now shared the back bedroom with my young Uncle Ernie. Only fourteen years older than myself, he had already been at work for ten years, a clerk in a coal merchant's office in Bedford Square. Pretending to be asleep, I watched him through half closed eyes as he got ready to leave the house, giving his jacket a final brush, pocketing some loose change and a packet of Players from the mantelpiece, clipping fountain pen and propelling pencil into a waistcoat pocket. From the top of the chest of drawers he would select a clean white handkerchief.

Although we had never seen the office where he worked it was familiar to us from his frequent description: the winding staircase rising up through the large Georgian house, from the very top of which he had once dropped an armful of heavy ledgers which fell straight down the stairwell to the basement, (causing what damage on the way we dared not think of). Busy rooms off each landing, each with perhaps a small square of carpet on the linoleum, and in winter a coal fire burning in the grate. Upright pedestal telephones. An office manager's roll-top desk. Enormous metal safes. Inkwells and blotting paper. In every corner a hat-stand and a place for wet umbrellas.

Even the staff were known to us by repute. There was old Gow, the office chief, of unpredictable temperament. Young Mr John, the chairman's son, who sometimes popped his head round the door with a query on say the whereabouts of a special delivery of ten tons of Welsh coal in the charge of the Great Western Railway. The office flapper 'Mac' who had a lot of cool cheek, but was really not a bad sort under it all. Harry Fortens, a dried-up sort of man who kept his own counsel. And the volatile Miss Boffey, given to long periods of offended silence.

Later, when the bedroom was clear, my grandmother having made the beds, would tidy the room up, perhaps replacing newly washed and ironed items in the chest of drawers. There was also a dresser in the room, a relic from the days of the lodgers, which now contained a lot of unrelated odds and ends – old wooden curtain rings, a set of dumb-bells, a defunct cat's whisker wireless set, old papers and postcards, a few Sunday School prizes from years gone by. The room was occasionally used by my grandfather, if he found it necessary to make a special 'pen' for his work the following day. Such items were fashioned from a malleable sheet metal he called German Silver. For one performing quite a skilled task, he seemed to work in rather an absent-minded fashion, using whatever tools came to hand, the kitchen scissors, an old knife, some pliers from the dresser. Puffing away at his pipe he was all the time full of talk on whatever vital topic was exercising his mind at that moment – the League of Nations, Organ Music, the threat from the Bolsheviks, the corn colour of his wife's hair when they were first married.

My mother has appeared only sparingly so far in this narrative. Now perhaps is the time to fill in some details of her own life, so closely interwoven with my own as a child, and indeed for many following years. As Lilian Mary Buck, she left school at fourteen, in the early years of the century. She was a bright, intelligent girl, not especially successful scholastically, but clever with her hands.

As a child, a great treat was to be given a bundle of assorted scraps of fabrics, perhaps a remnant of lace, velvet or silk, to be sorted over and made into clothes for her dolls.

She was apprenticed to dressmaking at Boardman's, a large departmental store in Stratford. In those early days, before the First World War, while a growing proportion of women's clothes were for sale ready-made, many women still preferred their clothes individually tailored, either by a local dressmaker (someone 'round the corner') or, in the case of ladies of more affluence, from a professional salon. The elaborate fashions of the late Edwardian period demanded a prodigious amount of labour in the making of just one garment. Moreover, workrooms were often in the charge of some martinet demanding meticulously high standards – offending sleeves would be ripped out in front of the unfortunate seamstress, who would be subjected to vilification. The girls worked long hours, 8 till 8 on weekdays with breaks for lunch and tea. Saturdays, 8 till 4. Apprentices only received a shilling or two for their week's work, which commenced with prayers under the glass dome of the fashion showroom.

Shaving in the Scullery

Despite iron discipline and exacting work, my mother enjoyed her years at Boardman's. In the course of time she emerged as a skilled and trusted operator, assigned to cutting out the often very expensive fabrics into shapes evolved from paper patterns she had herself produced. She was inventive, and had a bright creative mind. Like all her contemporaries in those pre-war days, she went to church on Sundays, attending the Congregational Chapel in Balaam St, Plaistow, characteristically furnished with an enormous gallery, ample space for the hundreds of young people who flocked to worship. Sunday evening was a time for dressing up, the girls in their seasonal finery, the young men in sober suits and spotless stiff white collars.

My mother had many admirers in the ranks of these young men. Then Percy arrived on the scene. Percy Dawson and his older brother Norman were not long returned from a year or more in Canada and the United States. It is not clear by what means Percy became a qualified engineer; on the outbreak of war he enlisted in the Ordnance Corps with the rank of Staff Sergeant Artificer, a position he retained throughout his service. I have in my possession two of his war-time notebooks. They are models of precision and clarity.

The Cantata

Percy was a go-getter. Perhaps his transatlantic experience helped. Having introduced himself to my mother, and, I do believe, declared there and then his intention to marry her, by his persistent but thoughtful attentions gradually melted away any initial reserve she may have felt towards him.

They were married at Easter 1917. It was bitterly cold. During the early part of the war, while stationed in France but still reasonably close to the English Channel, Percy had often taken week-end leave from his unit, and he and Lily had been able to spend Sundays together at Dover. (My mother used to say how welcome, on her late-night return to Forest Gate, was the sight of her father waiting patiently at the station ticket barrier, to escort her home through the darkened streets). But in the months preceding the wedding they had been unable to meet. Consequently my mother made all the arrangements for the ceremony. Percy was to arrive at his mother's house late the previous night, and by custom would not see his bride until they met in church on their wedding day.

He was late arriving at the church. Not just a little late, but seriously late. When he eventually arrived, my mother, in a turmoil of conflicting emotions, went ahead with the wedding, but in a mood far from the joyful relaxed condition she had anticipated. Earlier it had been agreed that following a reception at my grandparents' home, the honeymoon would be spent at Mrs Dawson senior's house, with the newly weds spending time on their own in London, or visiting friends. It now emerged that Mrs D (regarded by the Bucks at best as somewhat eccentric) was the culprit in her son's late arrival. He had arrived home the previous night exhausted by 24 hours' travel across France. She had allowed him to sleep on in the morning, recklessly eroding the time needed to get to church. When later, after the party, they arrived at their honeymoon lodging they discovered their small bedroom aglow with the light of a welcoming fire, a full scuttle of coal standing by in the hearth. This almost unheard of concession (normally reserved for the direst of emergencies) had been prepared and lit by a perhaps penitent mother-in-law. All was forgiven.

Percy's death from wounds in September 1918 was the price one family made towards the prosecution of the war. For four years this price had been exacted in millions of homes throughout Europe. Two months later the war was over. Germany sued for peace. The Armistice was signed on the 11th November 1918. The killing had stopped. Twelve days before the Armistice, at the end of October, Lily had given birth to a son. There was of course no radio in those days. The news of the end of the war was spread about by thousands of paper-boys charging through back streets shouting out the headlines. When the news reached Beauchamp Road it was received by Lily's mother. Lily was upstairs, resting with her new-born son. Her mother hesitated in breaking the news to her, but at length entered the room and quietly announced that the war was over. Years later my mother was to say to me: "I pretended to be unaffected; I was not going to let her see me cry."

To a young child, the environment in which it finds itself is accepted without question. That my mother was a war-widow was a fact of life; no secret was made of my father's death. I was familiar with his wristwatch, the worn leather strap, the hinged metal disc which when closed concealed any glimmer of light from the luminous dial, the medals. Best of all was the small scale model of a Sopwith Camel, the fighter aircraft of 1917, its wings cut from sheet brass, the fuselage of aluminium with the coloured RAF roundels painted in position. But for adults, they must find the wherewithal to live. Money. My mother now had to exist on a war-widow's pension, with a 10/- supplement for her dependant son. In all, just over £2. Not a fortune. Much as she would have liked to lead a separate life in her own home, there was no practical alternative to continuing to share with her parents: they willingly set aside two rooms. But she was determined to pay her way. She took in dressmaking. The exercise of her undoubtedly considerable professional skills, apparently an ideal solution, turned out to be a trap. The expertise and hard work put into each garment was poorly rewarded, she charged very little to her customers, producing finished items made to their own measurements, sometimes individually designed, to a higher standard by far than that offered by local shops. The margin of profitability was so low that my mother sometimes found herself working night and day for virtually no return whatsoever. She also was concerned by the lack of time spent with her young son. Her young son strayed.

A small green gate had at some time been inserted in the fence that separated the back gardens of numbers 6 and 8 Beauchamp Road. Getting through it was a tight squeeze for an adult, but presented no obstacles to a four-year-old boy. Passing through, I entered into a delightful new environment, a tessilated path beneath my feet framed by an enclosed arbour of greenery, a tunnel of climbing roses - Princess Alexandra and American Pillar - and a profusion of unwinding ferns.

All was calm and serene. Gone, the workday bustle of No.6. (Two apprentices together with Elsie had joined the dressmaking enterprise in the backroom. It was all machining, sewing, pinning, marking out fabrics with a little spiked wheel, then cutting it out, several hot irons, tacking, fitting. My mother thundered up and down the stairs two at a time). One of my great-aunt's treats in her green oasis was her delicious homemade lemonade. This was served from a pottery jug into quite elegant glass tumblers with fluted sides. It was kept deliciously cool by being stored in the cellar where it stood in a zinc fronted food safe, its contents protected by a small muslin cover weighted with china beads. Equally delectable to my mind was the lovely lemon-flavoured drink made from Monk and Glass crystals. This was contained in a moulded glass carafe, with a large glass stopper. I spent quite a lot of time in No.8. "It's a wonder you don't go and live there" was the somewhat caustic comment from my grandmother.

Completing her rehabilitation, my mother, always interested in poetry and poetry reading, had enrolled in an Elocution course at the London School of Music in Earlham Grove, where her young brother Ernie was taking piano lessons. She discovered she had a strong, warm, expressive voice and a satisfactory presence on a platform. A treasure chest of poetry was opened up to her: Shakespeare, Milton, Blake, Wordsworth, the Brownings. She learned how to Project the Voice, the practical importance of Deep Breathing, the role of the Diaphragm, Stance, Deportment, Pronunciation. Thus an Elocutionist joined the other performers who entertained at our occasional front room parties. With additional chairs drawn from all parts of the house, a dozen or more friends and relatives would gather in the rosy gaslight, enjoying a musical evening. (They all came furnished with music cases containing sheet music; these hidden away modestly until by acclaim they were required to render an item). Refreshments were passed round, oranges, figs, dates, and assorted nuts. Glasses were ranged along the mantelpiece; a bottle of port decanted. After some coaxing Uncle Tom would sing *Home Sweet Home* in a beautiful rich baritone. Cousin Hilda followed with *Il Barce* in Italian (nudge, nudge). Elsie recalled *The Hills of Donegal* accompanied by Ernie on the piano, and Bob Folkes with his flute. Two elderly ladies offered the duet: *'What are the wild waves saying?'* A child calls out suddenly "COALMAN! " The pianist is convulsed, tears streaming down his face. Outside, in the hall, Polly, another sister of William and Arthur, a simple soul, having consumed two glasses of ginger wine, lies supine drumming her heels on the linoleum. "She has chucked her dummy!" is the unsympathetic comment from one of her brothers.

My mother began accepting outside engagements, reciting at church concerts and other social events. One popular favourite, often delivered as an encore, was

The Party in the Front Room

a comical child-study, delivered as a monologue but with piano accompaniment. This always produced waves of laughter. This then was the hectic life of 6 Beauchamp Road, in the early nineteen twenties. But fate had yet another blow in store. This time it revolved around me. At Christmas 1925 I was taken ill, the rapid deterioration of my condition causing concern. In and out of consciousness I spread considerable alarm and some despondency by enquiring, in an apparently lucid moment, who were those two people standing at the foot of my bed, with big wings like birds? Later I roused up sufficiently to declaim in a weak treble: "He threw her down, and bit her breast." My great aunt Alice, who was present said, "Wherever did he pick that up?"

It was pneumonia. And measles. In a coma I was admitted to East Ham Hospital, where I was placed in an isolation ward. Pneumonia was in those days a killer, particularly in children, the patient sinking rapidly until a crisis point was reached. Over the Christmas I am told my life hung in the balance. My

The Sunday School Anniversary, Woodgrange Baptist Church

mother visited three times a day; in the strict regimen existing in hospitals in those days, when she was discovered holding my hand, she was asked to withdraw and wash, thoroughly. But doctors and nurses were really most supportive; great interest was shown in my progress, and as I gradually improved my mother was warmly congratulated.

I took food again, and assured my mother that I would be quite willing to continue the hospital diet which included peeled grapes when I returned home. When at length this day arrived we departed in the luxury of a taxi (I was too weak to walk) with myself clutching a box containing a clockwork train set, a gift from Father Christmas in the Children's ward. Convalescence was to take three months, and when I returned to school it was for mornings only. In the afternoons we were out taking the wintry air in all weathers, well wrapped up, floating homemade boats and feeding the ducks on the lakes of Wanstead Flats. The boats were cigar boxes, their seams waterproofed with candle-grease, propelled by paper sails.

My mother abandoned dressmaking. She continued from time to time to make clothes for family and friends, but the intensive business was closed down, the apprentices gone. She would prefer to spend more time with her young son, resenting the industry of the past two or three years which had limited their time together.

Her aunt and uncle, Alice and Arthur, were stalwarts of the local Baptist Church. We sometimes joined them on a Sunday morning. Their pew was in a conspicuous position right at the front, under the eyes of the choir and with a good view of the organist, who apparently writhed in discomfort as she led the singing. When the sermon came round Arthur would produce some scraps of paper for me to draw on. On a good day he would let me use his silver propelling pencil, a great treat. These early oeuvres, attested as to age and authenticity by Alice, have somehow survived up to the present. Their subject matter was not too different from today's – trains and trams with passengers bustling about – but perhaps fewer airships now. On one occasion Arthur took me aside and earnestly advised me to chew each mouthful sixty times. He and Alice were among the first residents in Beauchamp Road to install electric lighting. The filament in these early electric light bulbs was contained in a vacuum; when dropped they went off like a bomb. Early failure rates somewhat extensive, Arthur kept a row of defunct bulbs, on a shelf in the scullery, handy for hurling at any stray cat trespassing in his tiny garden.

When I was five or six he appointed himself to conduct me to Sunday School, then still packed with children. On anniversary weekends in May, a concert would be held on Saturday night with items –songs, recitations, playlets – from the scholars. Prizes were presented for regular attendance and good conduct, and for successfully learning by heart prescribed passages from the Scriptures. On the Sunday, the church would be filled with flowers, and all the children urged to wear a buttonhole, lilies of the valley, pansies, or an early rosebud. As well as Sunday School Scholars, the Girls' Life Brigade and the Boys' Brigade would parade, led by their bands. It has to be said, that when the Boys' band opened up, all hell was let loose. All the remaining seats would be taken up by parents and regular worshippers. Special hymns had been practised, soloists organised, a visiting preacher engaged. The vast men's meetings of the pre First World War days were over where hundreds of men had packed the churches on Sunday afternoons, the singing often accompanied, in addition to the organ, by an orchestra, with soloists and special speakers. Only a small number remained, and these poorly attended. The survivors of the Great War stayed away.

Women's meetings, often held midweek, varied considerably in numbers. In the East End of London areas of extreme poverty became control points for the distribution of welfare – clothes, blankets and food. It was also common practice for churchwomen's groups to sew clothes and make other provisions for those in need overseas, supporting denominational Missionary Societies still operating freely in India, China, Asia, Africa and South America.

Baptism by total immersion

Sunday Evening in Upton Lane

The non-conformist churches were largely self-governing and autonomous, under the chairmanship of the Pastor. Each church maintained a wide range of supporting activities, Bible Study Classes, prayer meetings, a mid-week service, Christian Endeavour as well as Temperance observance (The Band of Hope). In the prominent area of youth work, the Girls' Brigade, the Life Boys, the Boys' Brigade paraded on a number of evenings; there were Gymnastic classes, and Young Men's Clubs.

Although a certain amount of larking about took place around lengthy and sometimes fairly dark corridors, the general atmosphere pervading public worship was of fairly concentrated religiosity, culminating in forty-five minute sermons of intricate and highly emotive theology delivered by the Pastor. (Later, during my war service, I had a High Anglican friend who derided the extemporary prayers of the non-conformists. He said he couldn't listen to them. We certainly exercised a wide range of our own religious clichés, "Thy manifold blessings" etc uttered with great solemnity and much protestation of unworthiness).

Proper holidays, involving lengthy travelling, were often due to the generosity of Alice and Arthur. We went twice to Shanklin, in the Isle of Wight, in the early 1920s. How splendid to go out into the sunlit streets before breakfast with sugar for the milkman's horse, to see the donkey treading the water-wheel at Carisbrook Castle, to dig the coloured sands of Alum Bay.

In 1929 we visited Minehead in Somerset. (Just before leaving we paid a visit to Shortland, the school outfitter in Woodgrange Road, and purchased items for my new school, a cap with red and blue quarters (2/9d) and as I was to be seriously involved with homework, a leather satchel (4/6d).) There were six in our party at Minehead, the number being made up by two friends of Alice and Arthur. Steve was a real comic, a marvellously funny man to be on holiday with, a joke for every occasion. By contrast Lena was fairly quiet in a pursed-lipped kind of way. She said that when they were on their own on a winter's night, it was difficult to get a word out of him.

Our holiday was memorable firstly for travel in a motor coach. We left Victoria early in the morning in pouring rain, peering dimly through celluloid windows, the canvas roof of the coach remaining firmly in place for the whole of the journey. At mid-day, lunch in a hotel in Salisbury; we arrived at Minehead in the early evening. The weather relented; a late sun broke through the clouds.

Our landlady was the apple-cheeked Mrs Boddy. The other four had stayed with her previously; she was a renowned and much-praised cook. We sat down at mealtimes to a dining table arrayed in spotless damask, a rolled stiff napkin at each place. On the table was a massive cut-glass cruet and a substantial water jug and tumblers (no alcohol on the premises).

The Pavilion, Southend Pier

The food was superb and in generous quantities, mid-day luncheons comprising say, a magnificent roast with all appropriate trimmings, and an abundance of delicious vegetables from the garden, to which we helped ourselves from matching tureens, followed by the most delectable puddings. The menus were nicely balanced. Thus if by chance a slightly less substantial first course was served (say a delicately flavoured local fish concoction) then this would be counterbalanced by some really block-busting effort, for example the famous and eagerly anticipated Damson Pudding. Noisy guests would cheer a flushed Mrs B as she triumphantly took the supreme dish to the table, accompanied by a bowl of the yellowest, creamiest custard.

High tea followed at about 6.30. Here perhaps a cold chicken and ham pie, a colourful mixed salad in a cut-glass bowl, plates of bread and butter, jam, a large china teapot with knitted cosy, extra hot water, milk, lump sugar in a blue glass bowl with silver tongs. A fine fruitcake resting on a crocheted doily on a glass stand. Further hot drinks were available at bedtime, and of course early morning tea on awakening. Jugs of hot water for morning ablutions were placed outside bedroom doors, with supplementary arrangements for shaving ... all this, plus a hot cooked breakfast was provided for two guineas a week.

Summer holidays. Matchless blue days, the sun glowing on our faces long after dark. Standing on the cliff, sea breezes tugging at one's shirt. Rock pools, their green depths inhabited by who knew what strange creatures, imprisoned until the next tide. Lovely yellow ha'penny ice-cream cornets. A kiosk sheltering under an enormous teapot; 'Trays for the Beach'. Paddling, with one's feet sinking into the shifting sand.

When we set out for the day's activities (usually mornings on the beach, afternoons exploring inland) we removed our walking sticks and parasols from the hall stand, Arthur pausing prudently to tap the barometer. Touring, in the summer of 1929, presented no difficulty, other than involving a modicum of pre-planning. You had no personal means of transport (unless perhaps a bicycle) but could travel in almost any direction on a criss-cross of local railway lines, relying on the unfailing punctuality of the trains. Where there was no rail link, local buses, also working to a timetable, were available. In the West Country, cream teas were to be had at countless wayside cottages, sometimes taken in leafy back-gardens, in the shade of ancient apple trees.

Alice and Steve carried cameras. It was important to record the sunlit scenes, later to be pasted into an album and revisited on a winter's night. Alice had a Box Brownie, eight exposures on a one-shilling film, developing and printing available from any chemist. Steve was more adventurous with a quarter-plate camera, with bellows, which folded flat into a mahogany case. This was more complex in operation as each glass negative had to be loaded separately, and allowances made for shutter speed and exposure time. For Alice, writing cards was a daily engagement. Cards with attractive views were despatched daily from her pen to friends in all parts of the country. (Her pen was an ONOTO, a fountain pen filled by syringe-action, with an impressive ink capacity). Cards could be posted for one penny. Like the trains, the postal service was swift and reliable, with several collections and deliveries each day. The recipients of Alice's cards would enjoy their contents at breakfast time the next morning.

THREE

In September, the new school.

"Mum, our headmaster is a doctor, Doctor Burness! (Not a proper doctor of course, like Dr O'Driscoll)"

"Mum, we are to learn French, and one of our teachers is a real Frenchman. His name is Cerisier, which means Cherry Tree. Everybody calls him that behind his back, that is".

"Mum, the girls PT instructress comes on a motor-bike! She wears BREECHES!"

"Mum, one of the masters is a clergyman. He teaches English and wears a parson's collar!"

The senior and junior schools lay in separate blocks, to the left and right of the Scholars' Entrance, in between a wide expanse of asphalt. Senior school comprised the lower and upper fifth and sixth forms, the School Assembly Hall, the headmaster's study and office. The Junior School accommodated forms II and III, the upper and lower IVth, the two gymnasia, the Old Art Room and science laboratories. We discovered that the distribution of places followed the order of candidate's individual success in the Entrance Examination. I took my place in IIC along with 25 other ten year olds, including eleven girls. Our form mistress was a Miss Riley, a young woman with a manner that today would be described as laid back. In a rather off-hand manner she instructed us to bring our Bibles to class the following day. More than half failed to do this. Ruthlessly prepared to show us who was boss, Miss Riley awarded each of the offenders 100 lines, to be on her desk at nine o'clock the following morning.

"Mum, I've been given 100 lines. Can I start them now, or should I wait till after tea?"

Next day Miss Riley received these offerings calmly. "Next time I give you 100 lines to do I do not want to see 'I must not forget my Bible' endlessly copied out in rows and rows. You will copy poems and essays from the literature you are studying. Do I make myself clear?" She did not bother to check if all had achieved the full 100, but tossed the lot into the wastepaper basket.

Our chief bogeyman, mine in particular, was the Physical Training Instructor, Sergeant Pritchard. In his 50s, but, lithe and alert, in immaculate cream sweater and flannel trousers, facially he looked remarkably like General Kitchener in that famous Great War poster ..."I want YOU!" An appearance let down a little by the eyes, which were rather of the poached egg variety. With a very short tolerance factor indeed, Pritchard would lash out retribution with anything conveniently placed a slipper, the cane, or a length of rope. He frankly terrorised us. "When you appear in my gymnasium you will dress in white shirt and grey shorts. I do not expect a specially cleaned shirt – your mothers have much to do. BUT I DO EXPECT YOUR PLIMSOLLS to be spotlessly white, it is your responsibility to pipe-clay them, I WILL NOT HAVE DIRTY SHOES! IS THAT CLEAR?"

At examination time, when PT was cancelled, he was called upon to invigilate.

The Pyramid, West Ham Secondary School

He appeared neatly dressed in an ordinary brown suit, with an old fashioned wing collar. He had a tendency to nod off during these periods, to be brought suddenly back to full consciousness by the crash of a pile of heavy books falling to the floor. Followed by suppressed sniggering.

Adaptable as all children, we soon settled down to this new routine. The whole school met at Assembly at nine each morning for an act of worship, masters and mistresses attending in their gowns. We sang from our own Hymnal, led by a small orchestra organised by the senior Music Master. The head read out a set prayer ("...that we may do always that which is righteous in Thy sight...") always the same; we dispersed to our classes.

Most of the instruction took place in our own form room, but we visited the science labs for chemistry and physics, and twice a week had sessions in the Gymnasium and Art Rooms. Always I found drawing my most absorbing occupation. Throughout my days at the school, I often worked for part of the lunch break in the Art Room.

My scholastic progress after the first year was rather bumpy. In examinations I came to rely on high art marks to redress poorer results in other subjects. The Art Room was new. Light and airy, it was situated in a new wing linking Junior and Senior schools. The long corridor was innovatingly hung with reproductions of impressionist paintings – Monet, Degas, Van Gogh, Renoir, Sisley. The white-painted Art Room was the domain of a young man fresh from the Slade, Rupert Shepherd. Only 21, tall and dark, he strived for a balance between freedom of expression and the maintenance of reasonable order, aims not necessarily synonymous. The customary dreary groups (hideously difficult objects like step-ladders, deck chairs and watering cans) gave way to more enlightened art projects. Pottery was introduced, with treadle wheel and kiln. For those interested in lettering, type-sheets were available, introducing us wonderful modern-looking alphabets with exotic names – Beton, Open and Bold, and the newly arrived (from Eric Gill) Perpetua and Gill Sans Serif.

But it was poetry that brought me first into prominence. Not writing poetry, but declaiming it. We were expected to memorise certain poems; we could be called upon to recite them in class. For my part, I took this material home to learn it, and my mother seized the opportunity of imposing on it the richness of her own newly acquired elocutionary experience. (Deep breathing, the Diaphragm, Vowels, Consonants, Clear Articulation, keeping the voice up, maintaining the rhythm, all brought into play). When it came to my turn to recite in class, it caused something of a sensation. This was no mumbled, hesitant, singsong delivery, needing prompting, but a small child with a big voice, word perfect, expressive and apparently quite confident.

A stunned silence followed this performance. After a moment or two our teacher left the room, returning shortly with old 'Jumbo' Jennings, the senior English master. I was asked to stand up and repeat the recitation for his benefit, which I was pleased to do. Both teachers listened intently, with entirely straight faces. I was thanked, and 'Jumbo' retired without further comment. But it marked the start of my involvement in many school dramatics.

We were both eleven, and from the same form, although I was in the 'B' class and Hazel in 'C'. On Saturdays Hazel attended a school of dancing, and could tap-dance as well as sing and recite. She was a pleasant child with an even temperament, nice looking, very direct and quite un-shy. I myself had visited the Magenta School of Dancing in Barking Road, but only once or perhaps twice. The main studio had a shiny floor with gilt chairs and a stage at one end with a black upright piano and a gramophone. A globe covered with tiny mirrors hung from the ceiling.

For the school concert it had been decided that our form would enact *The Pied Piper of Hamelin*. Hazel and I would between us narrate the whole of Browning's poem; while behind us on the stage the action would be mimed. When the night arrived the School Hall was completely full. In front of the stage the school orchestra played a rousing overture, which was vigorously applauded.

Hazel and I stepped through the curtains and took our places on either side of the proscenium. I could not at first see through the glare of the bright lights, and when I began to speak my words seemed to hang in the almost tangible black air.

"Hamelin Town's in Brunswick.

By famous Hanover City"

The curtains parted to reveal the townspeople of Hamelin, headed by the Mayor and Corporation, all concerned with a terrible problem. "Rats," we recited.

"They fought like dogs and killed the cats, and bit the babies in their cradles".

Then the resplendent Piper entered, with his promise to rid the town of rats for 1000 Guilders. The bargain having been struck, the Piper started to play, and the rats came tumbling out. The rats were of course children dressed in grey rat's costumes complete with big ears, whiskers, and long tails.

At this point gusts of laughter welled up from the audience at the antics of the rats.

"...out of the houses the rats came tumbling:

Great rats, small rats, lean rats, brawny rats,

Brown rats, black rats, grey rats, tawny rats,

Grave old plodders, gay young friskers,

Fathers. Mothers, Uncles, Cousins

Cocking tails and pricking whiskers..."

The laughter took the narrators completely by surprise. Nobody had laughed at rehearsals. Well trained, word perfect, in full song, we never the less paused magnanimously so that none should lose our discourse – we knew we had to be heard above the shuffling of the rats (who had themselves been told to move silently, and above all not to talk to each other, but some of them were now grossly over-acting).

The Pied Piper of Hamelin, West Ham Secondary School

The poem ran its course. The Mayor and Corporation cheated the Piper over his reward; in return he played a different tune on his pipe, and this time all the children came tumbling out (no costume problems, here) to follow him into the side of a mountain, and were swallowed up forever. Hazel and I joined hands, and bowed to the audience.

On another occasion, I was selected to recite at the school prize giving in West Ham Town Hall. The poem was *Tarantella* by Hilaire Belloc. "Do you remember an Inn, Miranda, Do you remember an Inn?"

This may appear to be a slightly odd choice of poem for a twelve year old, but these were innocent days. In point of fact, in class I sat next to a real-life Miranda, a pretty, slim, fair-haired creature, the daughter of the then Chairman of the Education Committee. Miranda was bottom of the class, I the next. We never spoke to each other.

To a small child the excitement of going to the pictures was in the anticipation of something magical. Part of the build-up was getting there: short cuts through alleyways and fenced-in back gardens, then suddenly coming upon a main road with the cinema opposite. The thrill of actually getting in, the admission tickets whirring up at the Cash Desk. Carpeted stairs (covered with drugget if raining outside) brass stair rails, the closed double swing doors, inside the dark palpitating interior. Waiting behind the doors, a uniformed, scented usherette. Follow me. Torch illuminating the floor, past row after row. There, flashing on vacant tip-up seats. Edging along, people standing to let us pass. "Can you see all right?" The moving screen, enormous images. They speak in stentorian tones, with American accents.

The talkies had arrived by the very end of the nineteen twenties. The paradox of the cinema was that it deployed a realistic medium to present fantasy and unreality. Patrons (the cinema's own term) wanted to get away from the grey world outside, they sought ROMANCE, stories interspersed with the thrills of tension and violence, laced with comedy. Films that always ended with the hero and heroine in a passionate embrace; they lived happily ever after.

Some cinemas were enormous. In Stratford, the Broadway cinema which opened in 1927 seated 3000. In more or less the same area, a similar sized Carlton opened in Green Street, Upton Park. In West Ham at this time there were no fewer than seventeen major cinemas. As temples of unreality, it was appropriate that as the thirties progressed, many cinemas were decorated internally with lavish and fantastic designs, modelled in plaster and picked out in gold, silver and a plethora of exotic colours. Thus at the Broadway, above the proscenium and at either side were extravagant reliefs of romantic locations; as the programme commenced and house lights faded, these scenes remained illuminated for a few seconds more, myriads of stars shining in the darkening skies.

To keep these establishments full, with every seat occupied, more and more spectacular presentations were devised. In addition to the film content of the programme, management now added lavishly produced stage shows, often headed by some radio personality -a sure 'draw' in those days. Most memorable were the hour-long appearances of the famous Dance Bands of the day, themselves with legendary followings on the radio. The Show Bands Hylton, Payne, Cotton, appeared in the East End playing to rapturous audiences. Each playing distinctive 'Signature Tunes', the music was "faded in" in the style of a broadcast, the curtains sweeping open to deafening cheers as the band got to full volume.

The bandsmen usually wore some kind of uniform, but the real personalities, the leaders, whatever immaculate evening dress adorned their West End habitats, appeared before us in business suits, with rows of fountain pens in their waistcoat pockets. The programmes were varied with 'comedy numbers', in which some instrumentalists left their seats to act out some outrageous tomfoolery, wearing funny hats. Gales of laughter and applause. All this, plus two feature films. For 7d, 1/-, 1/6 and two shillings. Three times a day. To the small child returning home, the alleyways so full of excitement on the outward journey, had returned to a grey reality. Now dark, they were illuminated sparsely by occasional lampposts lit by gas.

At home, my grandfather had left Waterlows, and now had a similar job locally. He had curtailed some of his more exuberant activities; he no longer swam regularly with the Club which met at the Boating Lake in Valentine's Park, Ilford, an early morning routine (all out by 8am) followed every Sunday throughout the year, rain or shine, fog, frost, ice, or snow.

Now in his sixties, he had developed the trait common to many talkative people of advancing years he continually repeated himself. Thus his family gained an almost word-perfect knowledge of his fund of funny stories.

The Intermission, The Broadway Cinema, Stratford

On hearing one for the umpteenth time, we were sometimes unkind enough, while he paused nearing the end, for dramatic effect, to slip the punchline in for him. He would ignore these ignorant interruptions, proceeding single-mindedly to the denouement, often accomplished amid his own laughter, as if seeing the comic aspect of the story for the first time.

See what you think of this one:

An enthusiastic but distinctly uncouth young man was a new convert to the Salvation Army. He was taken with the band to an open-air meeting, and given the bass drum to beat. Called upon to deliver his public testimony, his acceptance of Jesus and his renunciation of a sinful past, he climbed on to the soap box and flung his arms wide to the small crowd gathered around, "Oh, my friends, my friends! Since I come to find the Lord Jesus, I am so 'appy... so 'appy...I could bust this bleeding drum!" (Is there something Shavian about this story? *Major Barbara?*).

To the social historian the nineteen twenties and thirties have their own separate identities. But for a child living through the time, life progressed from day to day, a continuous unfolding sequence of events. The twenties have been labelled the era of disillusionment, of social upheaval and strife, the period of the False Dawn. The thirties and with them my emergence into teen-age years were a time of change, of threats and anxieties, of the menacing future of war. The

The Redhead in the Lower Fifth

closely knit interdependence of family and neighbourhood friends showed the first signs of strain. So much more was now available outside the home; from within radio captured and entertained millions who would previously have drawn on their own resources.

All the time, I drew. I filled countless two-penny drawing books from Woolworth's, mostly with untidy scribbles in pencil or with pen and Indian ink. My subjects were cars (the latest models), trains, aeroplanes, airships all teeming with figures. I liked 'modern things' and was aware of the dramatic changes taking place in the World of Art. My first close-up experience of Modern Art was provided when, at the age of 13 or 14, I attended the first public exhibition of my young mentor, Rupert Shepherd, at a gallery in Bond Street

I was astonished by what I saw. My school was there, but not as I knew it. It was turned on its head. Stratford, Maryland Point and the Mile End Road, those well-known landmarks were depicted, but seen in a chaotic travesty of their normal homely familiarity. All perspective, that carefully nurtured and elusive skill, was abandoned. Proportions thrown out of the window. Colour washes no longer under control, but sloshed on the paper with vigorous abandon. It was intoxicating. All those studiously assimilated skills down the plughole. As the popular Cole Porter song of the time had it"..Anything Goes!". How many more of our traditional attitudes were at risk? Could we really paint anything at all we liked?

Our second year at the Secondary School commenced the broad curriculum we would follow for the remainder of our school days. Form III B, in which I now found myself, was designated a science class, with emphasis on Chemistry and Physics, including French and German as foreign languages. Form III A, the highest achievers, became classical scholars, retaining Latin, Geography, History and English. Behind us were C and D classes.

We had a new Form Master, an enormous but gentle man named Bayliss. Opposed to enforced discipline, he preferred to teach us by reason rather than rote, the decisions affecting our class work being made by common assent, not imposed. The inherent weakness in this standpoint rapidly became apparent in the behaviour of the youngsters in his charge he was played up rotten. It was quickly noted that he had a large mole (or something) on the top of his head which became the subject of much derisive comment.

Decisions by general assent in practice were seen as long and boring discussions until someone made the contribution that coincided with Bayliss' already formed opinion. Thus if, say, we were to cast a play reading he would call for nominations as to who was to play some particular role, and allow all suggestions until at length (it had to happen) somebody would call out "Spittle" (this was the name of one of the boys) who was his favourite anyway. He would then claim that Spittle's name had emerged by common consent, and end the discussion.

He taught us German, and in contrast to our French lessons which were brisk and business-like, and confronted head-on problems like irregular verbs (we had to learn them) German lessons under Bayliss were regarded as 40 minutes of ennui, to be enlivened by ragging on a scale only just inside the limits. Even his bicycle came in for derision, a really antediluvian machine whose primitive brakes descended directly onto the rubber tyre, rather like a child's fairy bike.

But he tried. One summer Saturday afternoon the entire form was invited to tea at his home in Buckhurst Hill. The proceedings commenced inauspiciously for me, when, on the bus journey, in front of nearly the whole form I asked the conductor for a half-fare to the Bald Headed Stag, when I should have said the Bald Faced Stag. Contemptuous laughter. Bayliss' wife turned out to be German and had gone to a lot of trouble preparing an interesting menu of German savouries and cakes. Foreign food was highly suspect in the minds of twelve year olds from East London, by unshakable tradition reluctant to try anything more exotic than eggs and chips.

Another time he arranged for us to travel to London to see a desperately obscure German film *Das Blaue Licht*. This experience was spun out over several periods afterwards picking out what happened (in German) and, the phrases employed. He should have taken us to see Marlene Dietrich in the *Blue Angel*, a German language version of which was probably showing about this time.

A real tartar was the senior Physics master, a volatile and unpredictable character named Rigby (Old Joe). An absolute martinet, sarcastic, sardonic, he punctuated his lessons by demanding that all understood the point under consideration, should, on the cry, "WHO AGREE?" raise all hands in confirmation. He would then treacherously turn on some poor simpleton to explain what he had just agreed to.

English and History were favourite subjects. The history teacher was a very modern-looking tall man called Ridgeley, who had long sideboards and wore very wide trousers and double-breasted waistcoats. Occasionally indulging in sardonic comments, most of his energies were channelled into chalking up the most thorough notes on the period being studied, which we had to copy into our own exercise books. At exam times he covered acres of blackboard space throughout the school. Cramming. But effective.

English had commenced at rather a gruesome level with the reading of Milton's *Paradise Lost* (the images of hell remain clear to this day), followed by *Paradise Regained*. In later life one had some sympathy for Robert Graves' fictional portrayal of Milton, as a narrow-minded bigot, vindictive and priggish, and suffering from chronic constipation. We studied a new Shakespeare play each term, and enjoyed incursions into the splendid *Golden Treasury of Verse*, particularly identifying with adult pleasures yet to be savoured, romantic stirrings in twelve-year-old breasts.

On Sundays, I progressed up the ladder at the Baptist Sunday School. Here too examinations were encountered, but scholastic standards were not so exacting, and I achieved good results in the Baptist Union Scripture Examinations. In church circles, at least, I was a clever boy. The Sunday School was conducted on open lines, 200 scholars divided into classes of perhaps seven or eight each with a teacher, grouped in succession in a largish hall, youngest in front, boys on the left, girls on the right.

From the platform the Superintendent conducted the I earlier part of the proceedings, announcing hymns and choruses:-

'Jesus loves me, this I know,
For the Bible tells me so...'

He added simple homilies on everyday life from which a moral could be extracted. When the time for the lesson arrived the classes closed round their leaders, ready to receive the day's scriptural instruction. On the boy's side the most popular class seemed to be the senior one, the thirteen year olds clustering eagerly round their teacher, a striking looking individual of great personal charisma. During the preliminaries (marking the register, etc) he laughed and joked with the lads, but the message itself was presented with great intensity and at a high volume which could be heard all over the hall. Although the boys' expressions glazed over somewhat, they remained quiet and well-behaved throughout. What was the secret of this success?

Some of the unattached ladies at the church were also under his spell. A distinguished looking bachelor of about forty, a professional man with a practice in Ilford, they clustered around him just as the boys in his class had done. On these occasions he became very animated, acting in a manner that can only be described as like the Principal Dame in a pantomime.

His Sunday class was the nucleus of 'The Club', a loosely organised if rather secretive weekly gathering of young males between 12 and 21, held during the winter on church premises, or in the summer in Wanstead Park. There was also an annual 'Camp'. Having joined this band, I begged to be allowed to go to camp. As I had not been away from home before, my mother, having made enquiries, felt that perhaps it would be a good thing to let me go.

The camp was held at Tankerton near Whitstable in Kent. I attended three times, and although at different venues, accommodation always comprised a wooden hut in the garden, or the back yard, of a Holiday Boarding House. We boys slept on straw-filled palliasses, our leader on an iron bed in one corner. Food was supplied from the house.

During the day we played games on the grassy headlands, bathed in the sea (I learned to swim), investigated the foreshore with its moored craft of all kinds, explored the harbour with its railway lines, trucks, berthing areas for visiting steamers. On the first night I was struck down with dreadful homesickness. I hated the uncomfortable sleeping arrangements, and lay abandoned and in despair on the floor in the dark. Adding to my misery there followed one of the camp's highlights – ghost stories.

After prayers (intense and voluble) and following a suitable pause, came the most diabolical, blood-curdling horror stories. Our leader probably made them up as he went along, not appreciating the quaking fear engendered in at least one trembling soul, cowering under his bedclothes. But I quickly became acclimatised. Next day, homesickness evaporated in the morning sunshine; at night the ghost stories merely provided an exciting climax to the day's varied activities.

On one occasion our leader was seriously upset, I believe by a chance remark from his brother-in-law, who was spending the weekend with us. After the departure of this relative on the Monday morning, our leader sulked for two whole days, remaining in bed, accepting food in gloomy silence. This behaviour cast a pall over our lives; we were very relieved when eventually his depression lifted.

The next play presented at my day school was to be Barry's *The Admirable Crichton*. This comedy examines the reversal of traditional social division when

The Band of Hope – The Magic Lantern

an aristocratic family, on a world cruise and attended by servants, is shipwrecked on a desert island. Crichton, in the title, is a Butler. I was cast as Lord Loam, the head of the family. I had a big voice and a reasonable amount of experience but was really conspicuously too small for the role; my children who were elegant and grown-up looking sixth formers, towered over me. (My partner of the Pied Piper, Hazel, was about my size; she played Tweenie, the scullery maid).

In the final act, all were to wear evening dress. In my case no clothes could be found small enough. Finally we visited a theatrical costumier established quite nearby, in Disraeli Road, Forest Gate. Our party was admitted by two men who surprisingly wore full stage make-up, matt foundations, rouged cheeks, pencilled eyebrows and lipstick. They had a comprehensive knowledge of theatrical requirements; the whole house was stacked from floor to ceiling with carefully boxed costumes from Lady Macbeth to Long John Silver. They even found something for me. Group photographs of the cast indicate a well turned out production, excellent sets designed and painted by Rupert Shepherd. Seated, centre stage is a grotesquely minute figure, moustached and bearded, hair whitened by clouds of chalk, wearing full evening dress and a stiff white wing collar a full inch or more too big.

My mother's sister Elsie had long since married Billy, her suitor of Brighton days. They now had three girls of their own, and made a habit of spending their summers at a tented camp at Shoeburyness, at the mouth of the Thames estuary. When August arrived Billy and family would adventurously set out from East Ham, all of them (Billy's elderly mother included) mounted precariously on his fairly ancient motorcycle and sidecar combination. Billy was a spirited driver in his leather helmet, goggles and gauntlets, making full use of an enormous convoluted motor horn.

All the children of Will and Mary were attractive in appearance, but Elsie was the only one who could lay claim to real beauty. With a flawless complexion and fine features she at the same time displayed a natural and unassumed gracefulness. Her three girls inherited something of their mother's looks, their fair hair bleached almost white in the hot summer sun. They revelled in the outdoor life. Naturally athletic, prodigious throwers and catchers of tennis balls, expert at cartwheels and handstands in marked contract to myself.

No earthly good at games, for me periods spent in the school gymnasium were full of anxiety. I particularly disliked all equipment work ropes and wall bars to be climbed, horses to be vaulted, beams to be balanced on. With little natural co-ordination I was frightened of falling off. I clung with desperation upside down on the Beam, with Sgt Pritchard dancing in attendance "NOW, PUT YOUR RIGHT HAND UNDERNEATH, NOT THE LEFT, YOU FOOL!"

On one occasion, at the conclusion of a particularly gruelling session, he called me over and had me stand to attention. He stepped around me, assessing the overall effect, making various fine adjustments. "Head up! - chest fully expanded! Arms straight down the sides, thumbs in line with seams of trousers, feet at 45 degrees..." There was a pause. "Come with me," he commanded. I followed him into the changing room, where the rest of the form were struggling back into their normal clothing. "You will stop what you are doing. I wish to show you something of special interest," He motioned me to resume my position of Attention, which I did, straining every sinew.

"The perfect physique," he announced, allowing the class a few more moments to admire this surprising manifestation of excellence. Following this incident, and for some weeks afterwards, I became widely known as 'Pritchard's Perfect Specimen'. But it was a bit of a mouthful and mercifully fell into disuse.

Christmas is a time for families. After Elsie and Billy had moved permanently to Shoeburyness, we frequently joined them over the Christmas holiday. Once there was snow; Billy produced ice-skates and a toboggan. We made snowmen and pelted each other with snowballs. Wonderful meals were prepared and dispatched; in the afternoon of Christmas day, to intense excitement, the lengthy ritual of the exchange of presents. Sometimes two or three of the girls would come back with us to Forest Gate, to spend the remainder of their school holiday.

What follows is an extract from my Journal of 29 December 1937. The scene is our kitchen in Beauchamp Road. It is evening, and grouped round the large kitchen table, are my mother with two young nieces Pat and Jean, then about nine and seven. They are engaged in making doll's clothes, my mother instructing. In the opposite corner my Grandmother wrestles with her weekly letter to her son Bill in South Africa. The letter has to be finished that night, as the weekly mail ship (CASTLE LINE) sails on Friday. She would have preferred a quieter atmosphere. The girls are not interested in me, as they think I am making notes about handicrafts.

MUM: You have to make holes here, see?
PAT: Oh yes, I know.
MUM: Then you do a seam round, like this.
JEAN: Auntie.
No answer.
JEAN: Auntie.
MUM: Yes?
JEAN: Auntie, will you pass me the scissors?
MUM: Oh! (passes scissors) Run this up here and gather it round the top turning. Here.
JEAN: Auntie, I've done two shoulders and a top side...
(And so on. Everybody is humming *Little Old Lady Passing* By, absentmindedly).
PAT: Finished this one.
MUM: Good, now you can do this. Back sleeves. Puff. Knot at the end.
PAT: I can't tie knots, Auntie. (No answer)
JEAN: Auntie, I've done two shoulders and two sides.
MUM: Oh that's good. Now hem this ...do it slanting and small.
PAT: Auntie, shall I do this tiny? (No answer)
Shall I do this tiny, Auntie?
MUM: Yes dear, very tiny.
PAT: I can't do back stitch very well. I hate it.
JEAN: Can't do what? Back stitch? I like back stitch, don't you Auntie? (Pause, Little Old ' Lady, etc)

Auntie, what sort of stitch have I got to do?
MUM: Running.
JEAN: Slanting or what?
MUM: Running.
JEAN: Shall I do it up the side? Slanting? (Pause. As before)
PAT: Where's Tiger?
GRANDMA: In the garden.
PAT:,. Auntie, have you got that green seat in the garden now?
MUM: No, all chopped up.
PAT: It was better before, wasn't it, Auntie?
GRANDMA: Oh no it wasn't.
(Second movement, *Little Old Lady*)
JEAN: Grandma, are you going to Sunday School on Sunday?
PAT: I've done that (repeats herself six times). Here's one end and here's the other end. I haven't done this one yet.
(Little Old Lady, a snort substituted for every other word).
JEAN: You're trying to think, aren't you Jack? Are you doing sums? (Oh! Help!)

Trying anything on with Sgt Pritchard was a bit like playing with a volcano. But it was known from experience that if he could be started off on some suitable topic, he might well go on gassing for half the allotted PT period. We were formed up in two ranks, awaiting the first command. Charlie Goff raised his hand for permission to speak.

"Well, what is it, lad?" (showing signs of impatience)

Charlie swallowed hard, then plunged in.

"Do you think it does you any good, sir?"

"Does what do you any good?"

Now for it.

"Well, you know, sir... SEX... sir?"

Sgt Pritchard remained silent. The fluid eyes moved left and right. He lowered his voice.

"The class will move under the gallery".

There was no sex instruction in schools in those days. It is just possible that Sgt Pritchard, as the keeper of our healthy bodies, had been given a discretionary green light to pursue the subject should the moment seem appropriate. (His class may have had doubts about his suitability on this topic of such vital interest to us all. He was considered so much out of touch with normal life that he might conceivably have some crack-pot theories of his own, hopelessly unhelpful. We remembered his interpretation of the Foxtrot, leaping about athletically from toe to toe-we might not have much personal experience of the dance, but at least we knew that it was performed with both feet on the floor). Under the gallery, we made an informal group. Those at the front looked straight ahead, assuming man-to-man expressions. Those behind avoided his eye, and nudged each other.

Sgt Pritchard stood with his back to the wall-bars.

"Does it do a dog good?" he enquired of us. This was indeed a new angle, and we murmured among ourselves.

In fairness to Sgt Pritchard, it should be recorded that as we got older and moved up into the senior school, his atttitude towards us mellowed considerably. He even got the names right of a privileged few; absolute discipline had instilled excellent responses in class, no shouting was now necessary, just a brief word of command sufficient. In private, he was at all times attentive and courteous. In fact in later life many former pupils regarded his influence as paramount in their school lives.

At 14, newly arrived in the Senior School, we were moving into a period of change, including conspicuous development in our persons. Downy hair appeared on the chins and upper lips of the boys, interspersed with varying quantities of spots and pimples. Constant sexual arousal, often at most inappropriate times (being bounced about on top of a bus could bring it on, never mind impure thoughts) tormented us.

Attitudes to the girls in our class did not immediately change. Dismissive exchanges between the sexes remained constant and unflattering.

"Shut your face, you half-wit!"

"Here comes the girl with the billiard ball forehead!"

"Old Mutton legs".

And many other insulting epithets.

The girls could dish it out, too. On one occasion Grace (admittedly in a flaming temper) said to me: "I'd like to punch you, you nasty thing. You and your ginger hair! And you've got pointed ears like this, and a long nose and a long chin and a skinny face. And dogs teeth." she ended triumphantly. In winter the girls wore a dark blue tunic with a sash at the waist and a broad white yoke-like collar, their legs enclosed in black woolly stockings. During summer they wore light print dresses in blue and green, with ankle socks. Although generally as dishevelled and ink-stained as the boys, sometimes when perhaps a head was bent over a schoolbook, or in the momentary turn of a cheek, there was a hint of promise just about to arrive.

In the mid-thirties, my great uncle Arthur died. My aunt seemed diminished in her loss, although outwardly retaining a brave warm smile. She kept up her wide correspondences, and increasingly, for a few days, left home to visit friends. At school we now faced the run-up to our final exam, the School Certificate. All lessons were geared to this approaching event. But it was not all work. In the Upper Fifth more urbane attitudes were supplanting former voluble noisy exchanges between the sexes.

The school had a large mixed choir of more than a hundred voices, presided over by the senior Music Master. Avuncular in appearance, sporting a sort of tidied-up version of the Old Bill moustache, Graham nevertheless stood no nonsense, and had, over the years, developed an excellent musical tradition in the school. The popularity of the choir was doubtless connected with the ballroom dancing sessions which were permitted in the Main Hall after rehearsals.

How I managed to get into the choir I cannot imagine, as I have never, then or now, been able to read music, or sing harmonic parts. We sang Edward German's *O Peaceful England* with its sweeping rolling harmonies; Sullivan's *Tarantella!* all movement and conducted at tremendous pace. And with great fervour, the School song:

The Tuck Shop

'Fond and faithful be for ever
All the thoughts we bear of thee ...'
The singing was accompanied by the school orchestra. We met at seven
o'clock on Friday evenings, the girls no longer confined to school uniform, the
young men cleaned up and freshly brilliantined. On the way to these rehearsals,
I usually spent two pence on a packet of five cigarettes, Weights or Woodbines,
one of which was consumed on the journey. No smoking was permitted on
school premises, but quite a lot, I regret to say, took place in the boys' lavatories
during the short interval which preceded dancing. While all the girls were fully
engaged as dancing partners, the boys were initiated into the strange male rite
of lounging around the floor as on-lookers, enviably watching the action, but not
caught up in it.

When the week of the General School Certificate Examination arrived, a
sense of fatalistic calm displaced the preceding weeks feverish activities of
swotting and revising. Nothing more could be done. Either we knew it, or we
didn't. As the final moment arrived, we sat well separated in the Main Hall, the
fateful question papers face downwards on our desks.

The questions revealed, the knowledgeable ones fell to work with a zest, pens speeding over foolscap pages, brains racing ahead to decide whether to answer three or four (either one sufficient). Timing was vital, to finish precisely at the absolute end of the two hours allowed. Those who didn't know the answers chewed the end of their pens. After the first horrible shock of discovering they could answer nothing, they anxiously re-read the questions in the hope that some marks might be retrieved if the question could be answered partially. Others, in desperation embarked on some trick question, apparently unconnected with the syllabus, inserted by an unfathomable whim on the part of the examiner ('Describe a table'). For these, two hours was an eternity.

I passed at the second attempt. My headmaster, to whom I appeared as a lazy devil to be constantly goaded into activity, growled at me: "What happened to your Matriculation?" and sped off without waiting for a reply. To this day I cannot account for my lack of industry during these formative years. When my imagination was captured, learning was no problem. But confronted with Physics, Geometry, Algebra, Arithmetic, Chemistry (an endless list!) a bird in flight past the schoolroom window would take me off with it, into a private world of dreams.

My mother decided to let me take up art, a decision no doubt influenced by my lack of success in almost all other scholastic areas. Her decision met with some opposition, given our somewhat precarious financial position, and by the widely held view that Art was no way to earn a living. And no pension! Following the conclusion of these examinations, as the end of our schooldays approached, the entire form celebrated with a week at camp. We travelled down to Dymchurch in Kent in motor coaches. The camp was a former Army unit, consisting of standard wooden huts each accommodating 30 or so beds. The girl's dormitories were strictly segregated but we spent all of the daytime in each other's company. Four teachers accompanied the party, rapidly affected by the silliness which is part of the liberating effect of such a holiday. We found, to our surprise, that we thoroughly enjoyed community singsongs, led by a formerly overlooked (by us) master called Harris.

"There were RATS, RATS, as big as pussy-cats
In the Store, in the store ...
In the Quartermaster's Store!"
No doubt this chorus had its origins in the First World War. Other songs we sang certainly belong to that period, including the poignant:
"There's a long long trail a-winding into the land of my dreams..."
There were songs with actions:
"Underneath the spreading chestnut tree
There she sat upon my knee "
And comic songs:
"Do you want any dirty work done?
Any dirty work today?
Here we are, ready and willing
To murder your mother-in-law for a shilling ..."
This flat area of the Kent coast contained, in our eyes, one unique feature the

Romney, Hythe and Dymchurch narrow gauge railway. Famous throughout the world, the trains, which ran on its miniature tracks, were drawn by working scale models of illustrious steam locomotives. In summer the railway operated to a timetable (people went to work on it) and accommodation in the covered carriages allowed two people to sit abreast. We travelled thus frequently, and in these enchanting sun-lit surroundings we began to see the girls in a new light. We relaxed in each other's company. With the girls in their summer dresses we laughed and joked together, the confrontational behaviour in school classrooms a thing of the past. We bathed. We climbed lighthouses. We explored the shore. Later in the gathering twilight, when we said goodnight it was in the re-assuring knowledge that we would all meet again in the morning.

After lights-out, the boys reached for their cigarettes. Exotic brands, de Reszke, du Maurier, Craven 'A', were lit up and consumed in the darkness. Over excited, young Crowe, without his pebble glasses, pretended to be a ghost, rising up from his bed wearing a sheet and emitting horrible groans. As he swept down the central aisle he caught his toe on a bedpost, his groans changing instantly to howls of anguish. A week later we arrived back at Tennyson Road in Stratford, disembarked from the coaches and went our separate ways.

Schooldays were over.

School of Dancing, Plaistow

FOUR

West Ham Art School was contained in the northern section of the vast, ornate, Italianate municipal building opened in the first year of the twentieth century, the West Ham Municipal College. The building also included the Borough's main Public Library (whose business in those far off days of which I write, was conducted in total silence). Diametrically opposite the Art School, facing Romford Road, was the Passmore Edwards Museum, a purpose-built (if miniature) museum in its design, incorporating a sweeping staircase leading to a circular gallery under a glass dome. Memorable among the exhibits of local flora and fauna and archaeological remains, was an apparently flayed torso, the exposed vital organs and arteries identified and painted in vivid and realistic colour.

The Art School rooms comprised a series of lofty first floor studios facing north, many incorporating glazed ceiling lights. Of the senior students about half were domiciled in the Borough, the remainder from further afield in the County of Essex. . After the purposeful and highly organised life at the Secondary School, I found the new regimen relaxed in the extreme. Classes were held between 9.30 in the morning until 4.30, with a break for lunch. There was an almost total lack of pressure. This was a DRAWING school; we started at the absolute beginning.

The Life Class

We drew everything. Wheelbarrows, rowing boats, gas stoves, assorted luggage, curly hat stands, deckchairs, drapery, storm lanterns. We also drew from the Antique from full size plaster replicas of ancient Greek and Roman statuary. At the same time the syllabus introduced us to the History of Architecture, to Anatomy, to Perspective. We worked in silence, on cartridge paper (ld a sheet from the Steward) with 2B pencils and soft india-rubbers. Occasionally our studio would be shared with a group pursuing some other activity, such as weaving, or dressmaking.

We opted to pursue one or more crafts. Available were metalwork, including silver-smithing, Cabinet Making, Pottery. There was also a Department of Painting and Decorating, whose master gave us a year's course in the design and construction of stained glass windows. Once a fortnight a day was spent in London, working at either the Victoria and Albert Museum in South Kensington, or at an historic City church. We would lunch at a local ABC, beans on toast, bun and tea for about 1/6d.

Some hints of a bohemian life-style were displayed in our Senior School. The girls (in a majority, here) divided between the frankly exotic and the simplistic, longhaired, smocked variety. The young men wore loud Harris tweed jackets with grey flannel trousers. There was a shop near the British Museum where woollen ties were available (at 2/6d), about the width and weight of a golfing stocking, which when tied, produced an impressively large knot. Suede shoes were desirable, but not always affordable.

We would discuss any subject under the sun, assuming unshakable attitudes on topics of which we had little knowledge and even less personal experience. The over - riding factor cramping our style was lack of money. But we did our best to look like Art Students. But was the life quite what we expected?

The scope of the syllabus covered almost every subject of benefit to the Art student. But it started at absolutely ground level. Bright ten year olds could have coped with it. We were intelligent mid-teenagers recently released from intensive schooling, and could have run rings round some of the tasks with which we were confronted. This elementary approach had a stifling effect on our creative urges. Any work remotely imaginative was relegated to a minor session and on the smallest size paper (one eighth of a half imperial sheet). But the policy of the school, as a first principle, to the exclusion of almost all else, was the exercise and assimilation of the skills of DRAWING.

In our second year, still in pursuance of drawing aims, we were introduced to the Life Class (that is, if we had demonstrated by the quality of our work, an ability to cope with this signal enlargement of experience). Nudity, like the school itself, did not live up to expectations. The unclothed figures posed before us were in many cases veterans of thousands of such sessions who could maintain a reasonable semblance of any given pose for 50 minutes without moving (resuming again, after a 10-minute rest). Their maturity presented the student with exemplary insight into anatomical detail and movement. What perhaps was lacking was freshness. To preserve some degree of privacy, a curtained alcove masked the entrance to the Life Studio. Within this area, on a raised stand, a register of attendance was displayed, containing the scribbled signatures of those participating, to be collected before the end of the session by a steward with a strongly disapproving expression.

The history of architecture is a fascinating and rewarding study. All around one are the sometimes all-too-solid reminders of past styles of building. Our study of the subject began with memorising, in considerable detail, three orders of classical Greek Architecture – Doric, Ionic and Corinthian. To this day I can recall the salient features (and differences) of these orders, but is this knowledge of really vital benefit? A question on this subject turned up every year on the Board of Education Drawing Examination. This I passed in my second year.

The fortnightly visits to sites of Architectural interest in London should have ignited our enthusiasm, since the itinerary included many of the capital's most important churches. This it failed to do. This failure may have been due to a lack of adequate support by the teaching staff. I cannot recall ever having attended a full-scale lecture, nor were we required to submit written or drawn studies in any serious manner, although comment may have been offered on site about the work in hand, often caustic remarks about its insufficiency.

Our youthful enthusiasms were reserved for the fusion of glass, steel and concrete, the brave new world emerging in the use of twentieth century building materials. Like the new Penguin Pool in London Zoo, by Lubetkin, or even the black glass Daily Express building in Fleet Street (with its surprisingly ornate silver and gold Art Deco entrance hall). But these were not on our list.

A craze for contract bridge had taken such a grip on some of our fellow students, that on arrival, at say, St. Stephen's Walbrook, they would immediately climb up to the most inaccessible point in the church (usually in the roof) and spend the day playing hand after hand of keenly contested rubbers, an activity surely not envisaged either by Ecclesiastic or Art School authorities.

The Sketch Club was the one outlet for students' original work. Each year some notable was invited to open our exhibition. In 1936 the celebrated poster artist Tom Purvis performed this rite. In the 1930's the publication of a new poster was a noteworthy event. The originality of the best work lifted this genre way above the sphere of mere advertising into a popular expression of people's art. The influence of modern movements, notably cubism, was apparent; the elements in some posters were assembled and presented like a Braque still life, the lettering an integral part of the design. We greatly admired the work of Edward McKnight Kauffer. Notable posters appeared for London Transport, the Zoo, Ocean and Air Travel (Cunard, Imperial Airways) and the excellent tradition of the Railway companies, on view at every station, to which Tom Purvis was a leading contributor. What he made of our work I cannot remember. He certainly did not have the look of an impecunious artist. Dressed in a smart business suit, he sported the heaviest pair of horn-rimmed spectacles ever seen in Stratford.

Given the opportunity, students were capable of sustained hard work involving innovation and imagination. The following is an account from my journal of 1937 of our preparations for the Sketch Club Fancy Dress Ball. It perhaps supplies some authentic details. Saturday Jan 22nd. An eventful day, the date of our annual fancy dress dance at the school, or to give it its full name -

"The Sketch Club Fancy Dress Ball". For the past week the Art School has been busy preparing for it. So much so, that the Painting and Decorating department have been nearly swept of their feet. They worked at it every day this week, and up till 5 o'clock on Saturday! Egersdorff James and I had a pretty busy time too. We'd had to build a trolleybus for the Stunt.

Well, Saturday morning dawned bright and early (we've had a very mild January) and the first thing I thought of on waking, was that I'd got to go to the School to finish that bus. Having bathed and breakfasted I set off arriving at 10.30. We worked until 1.15. Then hunger got the better of my good nature, and I slunk off home. On the way back it occurred to me that the best way to renew my exhausted brain and weary limbs would be to spend the afternoon in the Cinema. And I did too. Saw Laurel and Hardy, which put me in good trim for the evening. Dressing up was a bit awkward. I was going as a Cossack, or something, and I wanted to have a clothes line wound round my waist. But the devil of it was, that as the rope spiralled round it got cockled and twisted. The result was that every blessed spiral in that rope had to be sewn separately. It was a hell of a job getting it off afterwards. The costume consisted of an emerald green silky blouse, with spirals of orange and yellow ribbon sewn on, the clothes line already referred to, black velvet trousers and a sort of black skull cap, with some more spiralling ribbons.

I arrived shortly before 7.30 and there were only a few people present. The Hall looked very nice decorated with hundreds of balloons hung up in a net, and round the walls really large murals enlarged by some of the students from designs by three of us. The refreshments were nicely set out behind the swing doors at the rear of the Hall. We got started about 8. James was MC, predictably dressed as a Brakeman on some American Railway (Santa Fe). As MC he wasn't brilliant – the pauses were too long. Things were a bit slow until after the 'eats' when the old excitement began to warm up again. I didn't miss many dances - and oh! I nearly forgot! I was dancing with a dame from the school in the Spot Dance, and sink me if we didn't win it! First time that ever happened to me. But that wasn't all.

Soon came the Fancy Dress parade. Parkin, who had come as a ghost was by this time not feeling too good, in fact shivering like a jelly. Well, we all walked round and round and then we listened to the Mayor's (she's a woman) adjudication. First the women. Mrs Murchinson as "Little Old Lady". Second, Miss Marjorie Murchinson (her daughter!) - "The Boy David!" If I was that girl I'd be more careful about exposing that much of me at a dance, even covered with bottled suntan.

I got the men's prize. Now this was a real surprise for me. When they called "Cossack" I goggled. Kind friends pushed me forwards and the Mayor thrust 100 Players in my hand. Oh boy! 150 fags altogether for nothing! Immediately after this all the balloons were released, and in the excitement I missed the Last Waltz because while I was thinking about it, all the girls were bagged. What did it matter if my feet hurt? Well what did it matter?

Up the road from the Art School, in Stratford High Street, there were three theatres. The Borough Theatre, opened in 1896, one of the largest in Greater

London, was designed by the famous Frank Mitcham, and in its hey-day many well-known actors had played there, including Beerbohm Tree, Sir Henry Irving, and Ellen Terry.

In my day, it had fallen on bad times. In the earlier thirties, the one remaining glory was the annual visit of the Carl Rosa Company, featuring Gilbert and Sullivan operettas. Now it was closed, the interior gutted and transformed into a cinema, but with, at roof level, bits of the old terra-cotta theatre decoration still showing above the neon-lit facade. Here, from the pit I saw my first pantomime -Dick Whittington. We were crammed in behind the stalls seated on red plush covered benches, hemmed in by pillars and not being able to see very well. Small children enveloped in a confusing but delightful atmosphere of glitter and noise, peanut shells under our feet, a pervasive smell of peeled oranges.

Later, with my mother, we visited the West End shows. Fairly civilised queuing for the gallery on little wooden folding stools, under a glass canopy. For a couple of shillings or so, in such a manner, we gained admission (at matinees) to many of the outstanding productions of the day: Gielgud's Hamlet, an austere but thrilling performance, the set comprising only of a faceted flight of steps upon which, ingeniously placed and lit, the whole of the play was enacted. A beautiful production of *Twelfth Night*, all the sets and costumes in black and white (in reality silver, grey, off-white, charcoal) with only one character, conspicuously, in colour. *The Private Life of Christopher Bean*, with Edith Evans and Cedric Hardwick, J B Priestley's *Johnson and Jordan* (Ralph Richardson) the first of Priestley's time-warp plays, a metaphysical mystery in ordinary everyday speech.

Two other theatres were open in Stratford in those pre-war days. The Empire, in the Broadway, was a top-flight music hall run by Moss Empires, at which many celebrated entertainers appeared. Access to the gallery here (for 6d) was up endless successions of staircases, becoming less ornate the higher they reached, ending in the precipitous gallery, right up at the highest point of the auditorium, with a close-up view of cherubs etc decorating the ceiling, and an almost perpendicular descent to the floor of the stage. The theatre was destroyed by bombs in the Second World War. The second theatre, tucked away near the station, was the Theatre Royal, at the time a second rank variety theatre. The only one to survive the hostilities, it later became famous as the home of Joan Littlewood's Stratford East productions.

The tension underlying all our lives from 1937 onwards was the prospect of war breaking out once more with Germany. In April 1938 I recorded in my Journal: 'We had a big war scare three weeks ago, when Germany entered Austria. All the chaps at the Art School, indeed everybody I think, took it quite seriously, and we discussed which of the Forces we would enter (or in the case of the potential Conscientious Objectors, which prison). However, the crisis seems to have blown over, for the moment at any rate'.

Despite war clouds looming on the horizon, life went on. Here are some recollections of a shopping expedition in London in January 1938. Wednesday 5th January. Today an adventurous day. Shopping – the Sales with Mum. By train to Liverpool Street station, thence to Oxford Circus. First port of call was

Lyons Corner House

Liberty's; we spent an hour and a half inspecting stock and making purchases (very inexpensive ones). Mum bought a length for a dress in a bargain department. Can you imagine me, surrounded by shoals of fighting females. After a few more rounds in the melée, Mum again emerged triumphant, bearing before her a couple of yards of colourful fabric destined to become a summer dress. It was then half past twelve, I was hungry. So we adjourned to a Lyons. 1.45 and we again joined the battling throng. This time, Selfridges. By now I had remembered what I came up for some illuminating colours and an agate burnisher for manuscript lettering. Of course I had left the name of the shop I wanted at home. So I asked at Selfridges Enquiry place – you can ask then for any kind of information – and do you know, they knew all about the place, telling me how to get there, even writing out directions.

On the way out I inspected a special exhibit, Capt. Eyston's "Thunderbolt"- the fastest car on earth. By this time Mum, who had been buying wildly, hadn't any money left; at least she had, but she could not get at it in public. So we went to an ABC and when we had finished our tea and bun, she retreated to the Ladies Room and replenished her empty note-case... Fortified externally and internally, once more into Oxford Street's clamour and bustle.

I pushed Mum across the road to Lilley and Skinners, and by the way, there's a very smart shop for you – interior decoration carried out in satin walnut with horizontal dull metal strips, brown carpet and subdued indirect lighting. Shoe boxes nowhere in sight. We sank into ultra modern chairs and ordered shoes for the Lady. "Tan, please, and not too sensible." Served by a deferential gent; "Perhaps madam would try these?" She would, she liked them, quite casually, just like that. They were 35/9!

Now in our final year at Art School, we occupied the exalted Olympian heights which had seemed so remote and unattainable on our arrival only three years previously. Some of us spent all day on the premises. The conscientious souls with their sights on examinations, or advancement to a more specialised branch of the arts, had private study to get on with. For others, the gap between the end of the daytime schedule and commencement of evening classes was filled with a variety of leisure occupations, including, in the students' common room, bridge (a craze) or table tennis, and in summer in the adjacent public recreation ground, tennis and swimming.

Now early in the New Year, permission had been granted for dancing class sessions on Friday afternoons in the College great hall. Since only a dozen of us were involved, there was plenty of room. Folding chairs and one or two card tables were grouped near the stage, together with a floor-standing wind-up gramophone. This rather knocked-about relic of the 20's had a lid, which closed down, on the spinning turntable, and below, louvred doors, which opened to let out the sound. In between was a compartment containing some fairly ancient 78 r.p.m. dance records, a few of them still contained in yellowing protective sleeves. Emitted with continual accompaniment of crackle and hiss, the raucous syncopated tunes soon became familiar: *My Song of the Nile* (waltz) Jack Hylton and his orchestra, with Vocal Refrain. *OK Toots!* sung by the American entertainer Eddie Cantor, accompanied by Ambrose's Band. *The Wedding of the Painted Doll* Jay Widney and his Midnight Follies Band, vocal refrain by Sam Browne. The style was distinctly upbeat. We gyrated enthusiastically, attempting to keep time with the music. The uneven vibrato of the vocalists (it was almost impossible to distinguish between men and girls) declaimed the burgeoning of youthful love and romance. We put more french chalk on the floor.

Although we were basically learning to dance, there was no formal instruction. We learned from each other; the girls had the clearer grasp of the intricacies of ballroom dancing, but the boys were supposed to lead the cause of much initial confusion. The main problem for the males was co-ordination of movement, compounded by the panic of actually holding a girl in their arms, a tension leading to at least one youthful embarrassment, sweaty hands. Two of our number were most proficient dancers. They moved as one, feet effortlessly performing intricate side steps, turning, gliding, reversing. About the same height they were by no means a matching pair. Bob was chunky, with heavy horn-rimmed glasses and black brilliantined hair, his clothes slightly spivvy. A dedicated gum chewer. His partner Dorothy was willowy and graceful, her dark hair loosely arranged. They never admitted it, but we knew they were products of the Greengate School of Dancing. I danced sometimes with Dorothy; it was a stimulating experience. Her body pressed close to mine, pelvis thrust forward, the long-striding legs moving between mine; her hair brushing my face.

Mostly I danced with Jessica. As the weeks went by, we formed an adequate partnership, due entirely to Jessica's skills in following my erratic steps. We sat out in groups, smoking cigarettes, Gladys, Victor, Betty, Jessica and myself. Others came and went: at about six thirty the session ended, and we dispersed to our separate activities. During the evening session the school settled down to classes open to all comers, in addition to the full-time day students. On offer were general drawing and painting, life classes, and a whole range of craft activities -dressmaking and embroidery, pottery and modelling, metalwork and cabinet making. Day students sometimes opted for private study in an unused studio or classroom, taking advantage of an opportunity to get on quietly with some necessary revision.

In one such venue, desks were set out in two rough circles, one end lit, the other in shadow. I sat with my papers and Bannister Fletcher's *History of Architecture*, and tried to get interested. Jessica, who was studying for an Art Teachers' Diploma, would sometimes sit a few spaces away. Both of perhaps rather reserved dispositions, we spent most of these sessions in silence. At length the ice was broken.

"I find it terribly difficult to concentrate on this boring old rubbish for any length of time. You are much more disciplined than I am, I'm sure you know a lot more about this than I do". She glanced up from her notes, voicing her own ignorance in vast areas of the subject. I said, "Would it be a good idea if we could test each other's knowledge? Did she understand all these architectural terms? For example what was a Clerestory?" She told me.

As we talked the subject in hand receded somewhat, to be replaced by our own reactions to the supervision, or lack of it, exercised by those in whose charge we had found ourselves. "Old Clarkson is supposed to be looking after our Architectural History. But we never see him. Those awful old-fashioned boots he wears. On perspective I find him completely incomprehensible. Anyway, what useless rubbish it is to pinpoint the sun's position; if you have an instinctive grasp of perspective, working out cast shadows is not difficult".

Our conversation expanded to include wider observations, including impressions of other students and staff. A mild-mannered but outwardly saturnine teacher of general drawing Jessica had, on first sight, considered to be 'the villain of the piece'. I said I thought he looked more like Groucho Marx. At the concluding hour of nine, having enjoyed an unexpectedly stimulating period of private study, we collected up our papers and went home.

In subsequent weeks conversation started up quickly, we seemed to have a lot to say to each other so many views to be quite fluently exchanged. Even less architecture was studied. On one occasion Jessica was accompanied by another class-mate. The easy bonhomie we had established was temporarily disrupted.

Tea in the Parlour

Tram to Jupp Road Baths

The newcomer's only direct comment to me was: "Dawson, you use a gold rinse on your hair, don't you?"

Thereafter we were uninterrupted. We laughed and sat side-by-side sharing the art school's only copy of Bannister Fletcher, but rarely referring to it. I suppose we gained in some part an intimate understanding of ourselves. Once Jessica said: "I hate seeing my face each morning in the mirror. I would desperately. love to change it". She was in fact quite a presentable girl of average height with dark brown hair and a slim figure, perhaps not yet understanding how to make the best of herself, or just as likely, too hard up to do much about it. For my part, I did not know how to respond, and made no comment.

These shared evenings with their warmth and intimacy were a separate part of our lives at the Art School; at other times when we met, as we continually did in classes, we were certainly not strangers, but led quite independent existences. At Easter 1939 Jessica left to take up a year's study of Pedagogy.

When the summer term commenced, daylight now illuminated my private classroom. As usual, in the corridors and adjacent studios, evening students settled down to their varied activities. I was on my own again. But not for long. As if by arrangement, another girl appeared in Jessica's place. To start with she sat meekly and quietly enough sorting through her notes. In fact this one had something of a reputation as an 'enfant terrible', and normally knocked about with three girl friends of similar disposition, of whom she was the leading light. She was about Jessica's size, but there any similarity ended. She and her friends were fee-paying students domiciled outside the Borough (Chigwell and Epping Forest area) and displayed different attitudes from the homegrown varieties, who in general worked harder and more diligently. (But not necessarily with more flair). She stood before me. "Do you think I could borrow your soft rubber?"

Viola quickly revealed herself as having a totally different personality from her predecessor. To start with she had an unquestioning confidence in herself, not in an over-assertive way, but the hesitances so characteristic in Jessica were unknown to her. She was also differently presented. Sensible flat shoes had given way to moderately high heels. There were traces of lipstick. Also, she was a blonde. Not of the conventional roses and cream complexion; a pale smooth skin almost sallow in tone, with cool grey eyes. She was terribly spoilt, accepting as a natural order of things, any advantage that came her way. Conversation tended to be acquisitive, but she revealed a great sense of fun, if somewhat barbed.

A variation in the established routine arrived; after the class I walked with her to her railway station, through the lengthening summer evenings. One day, we met in the corridor in front of the lockers. She said: "Why don't you come round one evening, and see me at home?" To which I replied "What a good idea".

My turn now to walk to the station, to experience her daily journey in the steam train. The trains were really scruffy, smelling strongly of soot, oil and steam, with overtones of powerful shag tobacco. The carriages were divided into compartments by head high matchwood partitions with rudimentary access above for hand luggage. Hard seats. A notice saying: 'DO NOT SPIT Penalty Forty Shillings'. Stopping at all stations, a half hour journey. But anticipation is all. It could have been the Starlight Express.

I rang the bell. She answered the door, I entered the hall. Panelled in oak, with parquet flooring and scattered rugs. I was introduced to her parents: polite but guarded neutrality. (I had already discovered that meeting a girl's Mum and Dad was not quite like the carefree exchange of schooldays; one was regarded with caution if not suspicion, occasionally with barely concealed hilarity). It was decided we should take the dog for a walk in Hainault Forest. This quiet mild mannered mongrel, no doubt surprised at being exercised at this late hour of the day, gazed down uncertainty, seen through a fringe of strands of grasses, heavy with seed, as the light faded.

Other such visits followed. Viola's parents drove us through country lanes in the largish Austin. She and I shared the back seat, our laps covered by a quite superfluous travelling rug, beneath which we held hands.

Later, alone together, she asked me: "What will you do if war comes?" I replied that I would join the RAF and apply for training to fly a Spitfire. (This had been known to elicit responses like: "Promise me you will do no such thing! PROMISE ME!!) But not in this case. I turned the question back to her. She replied with prophetic accuracy: "I shall marry an American".

In what turned out to be my final visit, in mid August 1939, we had the house to ourselves. She asked me if I would like to see upstairs, and took me on a sort of conducted tour along corridors, through bedrooms, spare rooms, bathrooms, ending up in her own pad, not much bigger than mine in Forest Gate. But the furniture was newer, and the view from the window not of grey slate roofs and chimney stacks, but of luxuriant green foliage. There was a small bed not unlike my own.

We lost all sense of time. It became dark. Suddenly there was a crunch of tyres on gravel, the slamming of car doors. She shot up. "Oh my God, it's Mummy and Daddy!" Galvanised into action as never before, we desperately straightened ourselves and bits of the room and sped to the door. But too late. As we descended the staircase, there, in full view, were her parents coming in through the front door. We walked more or less straight out of the house. What could be said? It seemed better to carry straight on, with a some ridiculous parting line like, "Well, I'm off home then..." to which Viola instantly responded "I'll come with you to the station" and we hurried out.

Back home, gloom enveloped all. Some days previously Air Raid Shelters had been delivered, one to each household. These were now erected in our small back gardens, dug in with the bases three feet or more below ground level. All the flowers were gone: the pretty blue drifts of larkspur, bright marigolds and geraniums, pansies and snapdragons, all were buried under tons of soil, and in their place occupying the entire back garden from fence to fence, a hideous catafalque of newly turned earth, a dank smelly grave, a tomb lined with corrugated steel.

We each had a personal gas mask, in the event of war to be carried at all times. The prospect of war hung over us like a pall. In our homes, the windows were criss-crossed with sticky tape to lessen the danger of flying glass splinters. In public places barrage balloons appeared, trenches were dug in parks and playgrounds. Some semblance of normal life remained. The routine of going to work, shopping, housework, school, carried on, but with people's thoughts

Grandad's Piano

After the Dance

elsewhere. If we went to the cinema the newsreels were full of the German Army, always seemingly marching a hundred abreast, invincible, implacable. Shots of Hitler bellowing away, his words unintelligible, their meaning clear enough. As Mrs Corck, a friend of my mother remarked, it was as if there had always been war; the time between the wars we had looked on as peace, was an unreal dream.

Viola and I met again at the Art School. What pressures my last visit had placed upon her were not mentioned, but it seemed as if the war clouds built up around us had in some way entered into our personal relationship. She was moving away from me. Precipitated by some ill-advised but chance remark made by myself, a pent-up torrent of retribution descended on my head. No discussion was allowed; foaming with anger she turned on her heel there and then in Romford Road, and strode fuming out of my life. The break was final and complete.

By November 1939 I was in the Army, training with The Rifle Brigade at Winchester. Leave was granted at Christmas and the New Year; by good fortune the Art School Fancy Dress Ball was to be held on the New Year's Eve. I reflected that as a previous winner of the Fancy Dress prize, I was unlikely to get anywhere this year, although the King's uniform was still something of a novelty. With a brutalised Army haircut and wearing a uniform the jacket of which was a First World War pattern, I arrived about midway through the proceedings. As if in defiance of the war, or perhaps as a last fling to irresponsibility, the Ball appeared as decorative and bright as ever.

The hall was hung with inventive decorations made by the students, hundreds of balloons remained netted in the ceiling ready for the midnight revels. There seemed to be an especially large number in fancy dress, and I received much attention from both staff and students.

Among the visitors was Jessica; with her friend Gladys they had entered into the spirit of the occasion appearing as Charlie Chaplin and Buster Keaton, wearing dark suits with respectively, a bowler hat, cane and small moustache, and a straw hat with clip-on bow tie. Victor, swathed in bandages, his normally urbane features smothered in flour, represented a suitably horrifying Mummy (Boris Karloff). I sat with them and exchanged news and pleasantries. It was nice to see Jessica again after nearly a year. She was now a fully qualified Art teacher, but uncertain about pursuing her career in wartime.

A commotion was going in the middle of the floor. In and out of the revellers Viola pranced and cavorted, attended by a new leading man, the pair of them dressed up as Tarzan and Jane, and wearing very little in the way of clothes. (Unclothed areas were painted in gaudy suntan make-up). Quite unsettled by the apparition I left Jessica and her group and moved around the hall on my own, passing in and out of the coloured spotlights, skirting the dancers.

Old Mother Hubbard, Tom Pierce and his Grey Mare swept past, followed closely by Hitler and Cleopatra. After a time Viola left the hall for a few moments, and when she returned she passed by me, paused momentarily, but moved off without speaking. She rejoined the activities with renewed abandon. I remained where I was; the kaleidoscope of colours, the chatter and laughter, the pulsating music providing a surreal background to my isolation.

The fancy dress parade took place, the prizes awarded, then "Take your partners for the Last Waltz". As the dancers gyrated spotlights picked out the thousand descending balloons; coloured streamers were thrown. A rowdier element quickly destroyed what was left of the 'stunt' floats. Amid the debris of popped balloons, the revellers formed two large circles for *Auld Lang Syne*. A final roll of the drums, *God save the King*. It was all over. In a buzz of animated conversation, the dancers made their way to the large exit doors leading to the College Vestibule. I remained where I was, waiting for the crowd to thin out when I would make my own exit.

I became aware of a commotion, of someone shouting, or more accurately BAYING in the grip of some intense emotion. I seemed to hear the word "PATHETIC..." (following words lost in noise and confusion) then, bellowed: "HE DOESN'T KNOW WHO HIS BEST FRIENDS ARE..." (more indistinct baying – was it a drunk?).

Somewhat alarmed the revellers now parted for a moment to reveal the cause of the disturbance; unbelievably an almost demented CHARLIE CHAPLIN (alias Jessica) covered in streamers and still wearing the ridiculous moustache, shaking with emotion, and possessed of a terrible fluency: "BLOODY BITCH...COME ALONG GLADYS, WE KNOW WHEN WE'RE NOT WANTED..."(this was an attempt to gain support from the fearfully embarrassed Harold Lloyd and Boris Karloff). Then she saw me, still lurking in the background "THERE HE IS, THE..." (mercifully lost in the commotion).

They got her out.

That this dramatic outburst should have occurred at all was surprise enough.

Dancing on the Pier

That I was the cause of it was almost too unbelievable to take in. To be caught up in such a situation, when all I was doing was trying to keep out of the way, left me absolutely shattered. Unhappily, I reflected on my two-fold rejection, first by Viola and now by Jessica, romance and friendship, destroyed so dramatically like the burst balloons and tangled streamers littering the floor.

Perhaps Beau Geste (funny, how his name should come to mind at such a function) had it right after all, I meant that he lost himself in the Foreign Legion. I moved off into the darkness. I had the Rifle Brigade.

As the war progressed, our household was quickly reduced by two (Ernie and myself into the Army) followed in the summer of 1941 by the death of my dear grandmother. My mother and grandfather carried on together throughout the worst of the Blitz until Christmas 1944. Then, returning from a visit to Shoeburyness, he was suddenly taken ill on the journey, and died on the train. My mother was alone in the family house.

My great aunt Alice, (who lived next door) several years a widow, had been deeply troubled at the outset of the war. Never having owned a wireless set, she developed the habit of coming into No 6 to listen to the evenings' news, and later to Churchill's broadcasts.

In the summer of 1940 she left London to stay with friends in Devon. I was on leave from the Army, and saw her off from St. Pancras station. On our way through London we conversed like old friends. I never saw her again; within months she was dead, her final weeks clouded by accelerating physical and mental debility.

We are at war